JOKE BOOK

WHAT'S HAMM'S BEST KARATE MOVE?

The pork chop!

WHAT DID BUZZ LIGHTYEAR SEE ON THE STOVE?

An Unidentified Frying Object!

WHY DOES WOODY WEAR A COWBOY HAT ON HIS HEAD?

Where else could he wear it?!

PUFFIN BOOKS

Published by the Penguin Group
Penguin Books Ltd, 27 Wrights Lane, London W8 5TZ, England
Penguin Putnam Inc., 375 Hudson Street, New York, New York 10014, USA
Penguin Books Australia Ltd, Ringwood, Victoria, Australia
Penguin Books Canada Ltd, 10 Alcorn Avenue, Toronto, Ontario, Canada M4V 3B2
Penguin Books (NZ) Ltd, Private Bag 102902, NSMC, Auckland, New Zealand

On the World Wide Web at: www.penguin.com

Penguin Books Ltd, Registered Offices: Harmondsworth, Middlesex, England

First published in the USA by Disney Press 1999
First published by Puffin Books 2000
8

Set in Stencil/Berkeley Italic 16/19pt

Printed in the United Kingdom

British Library Cataloguing in Publication Data
A CIP catalogue record for this book is available from the British Library

ISBN 0–141–30747–1

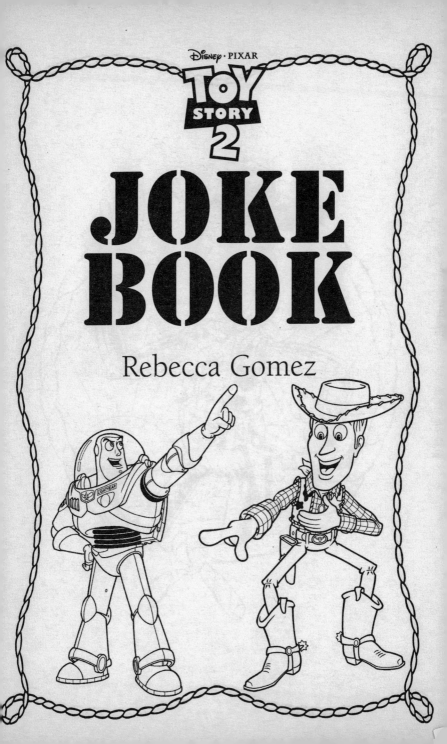

DISNEY · PIXAR

TOY STORY 2

JOKE BOOK

Rebecca Gomez

WHY DID ANDY CROSS THE PLAYGROUND?

To get to the other slide!

WHAT WORDS IS BUZZ LIGHTYEAR MOST AFRAID OF?

Batteries not included!

WHY DOESN'T MR POTATO HEAD LIKE FANCY RESTAURANTS?

He heard they cost an arm and a leg!

WHY IS SLINKY ALWAYS LATE?

He can't wear a wristwatch!

WHAT'S THE TOYS' BIGGEST FEAR?

Yard sales!

HOW DOES WOODY GET THE TOYS TO CALM DOWN?

He tells them to save their batteries!

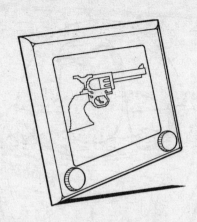

WHY WOULD ETCH BE A GOOD FRIEND TO HAVE IN THE WILD WEST?

Because he's a quick draw!

WHY SHOULDN'T YOU SWEAR IN ANDY'S ROOM?

Because there are preschool toys present!

HOW DO YOU GET MR POTATO HEAD TO STOP TALKING?

Take off his mouth!

7

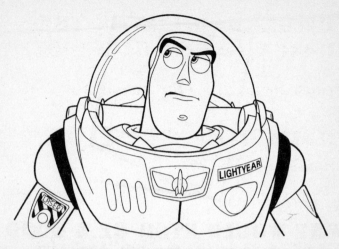

WHAT IS BUZZ'S FAVOURITE CHOCOLATE BAR?

A Milky Way!

HOW DOES BUZZ LIGHTYEAR LIKE TO TRAVEL?

Hyperactive hyperdrive!

WHAT HAPPENS WHEN MR POTATO HEAD IS SCARED?

He goes to pieces!

WHY DID HAMM GO ON THE MISSION TO RESCUE WOODY?

Because he needed a little change!

WHAT'S HAMM'S BEST KARATE MOVE?

The pork chop!

WHAT'S HAMM'S FAVOURITE LANGUAGE?

Pig Latin!

HOW WOULD HAMM WIN AT MONOPOLY?

He'd build hotels on Pork Lane!

HOW MUCH NOISE DID BO MAKE WHILE WOODY WAS AWAY?

Not one little peep!

WHO'S CLOSEST TO WOODY?

Bo. She's just a couple of blocks away!

WHY DID BO BLUSH?

She was feeling a bit sheepish!

WHO DOES HAMM HAVE TO BE WARY OF?

Pigpockets!

WHO IS HAMM'S FAVOURITE CORRESPONDENT?

His pen pal!

WHAT'S HAMM'S FAVOURITE BALLET?

Swine Lake!

WHY DO THE OTHER TOYS LIKE HAMM SO MUCH?

Because he's not a hog!

WHY CAN'T YOU TRUST BO?

She has a little crook!

WHY DOES BO CARRY A LONG STICK?

So she can be a cow poke!

WHAT DID PROSPECTOR SAY WHEN HE SAW BULLSEYE?

'Why the long face?'

WHEN IS BULLSEYE NOT BULLSEYE?

When he's turning into a barn!

WHAT DOES HAMM DO WHEN HE FEELS LIKE EXERCISE?

He lies down until the feeling passes!

WHY DOES MRS POTATO HEAD LOVE HER HUSBAND?

Because he's a real sweet potato!

WHY DID HAMM, REX, MR POTATO HEAD AND SLINKY CROSS THE ROAD?

To get to the other side!

Knock, knock.
Who's there?
Hugo.
Hugo who?
Hugo to Cowboy Camp this year?

Knock, knock.
Who's there?
Ken.
Ken who?
Ken I play with
Slinky?

Knock, knock.
Who's there?
Ben.
Ben who?
Ben to Pizza
Planet lately?

WHY DOESN'T BULLSEYE TALK MUCH?

He's a little hoarse!

WHY WOULDN'T SLINKY CROSS THE ROAD?

He doesn't have the guts!

WHO IS HAMM AFRAID OF?

Frankenswine!

WHAT'S HAMM'S BIGGEST FLAW?

He's a bit of a boar!

WHAT'S HAMM'S FAVOURITE HOLIDAY?

Valenswine's Day!

WHICH TOY SCARES WITCHES?

Mr Spell!

WHY DOES WOODY WEAR A COWBOY HAT ON HIS HEAD?

Where else could he wear it?!

WHY DOESN'T SLINKY LIKE PARTIES?

He has no body to dance with!

WHAT'S AS BIG AS REX, BUT WEIGHS NOTHING AT ALL?

His shadow!

WHAT IS BUZZ LIGHTYEAR'S FAVOURITE NUMBER?

Infinity!

WHY DOES BO LOVE WOODY SO MUCH?

Wooden you?

HOW WOULD HAMM GET TO THE HOSPITAL IF HE WERE HURT?

In a hambulance!

WHAT DO YOU GET WHEN YOU CROSS BUZZ WITH PROSPECTOR?

Someone who looks for gold in space!

WHY IS MR POTATO HEAD SUCH A GOOD FRIEND?

Because he'll always lend you a hand!

WHAT DO YOU GET WHEN YOU CROSS ETCH WITH BULLSEYE?

Pictures of horses!

WHAT DO YOU GET WHEN YOU CROSS SLINKY WITH A DOZEN EGGS?

Pooched eggs!

WHAT DO YOU USUALLY FIND IN REX'S MOUTH?

His teeth!

Knock, knock.
Who's there?
Rex.
Rex who?
Rex some more toys, Sid?

Knock, knock.
Who's there?
Howie.
Howie who?
Howie going to get Woody back safely?

Knock, knock.
Who's there?
Canoe.
Canoe who?
Canoe imagine
being one of
Sid's toys?

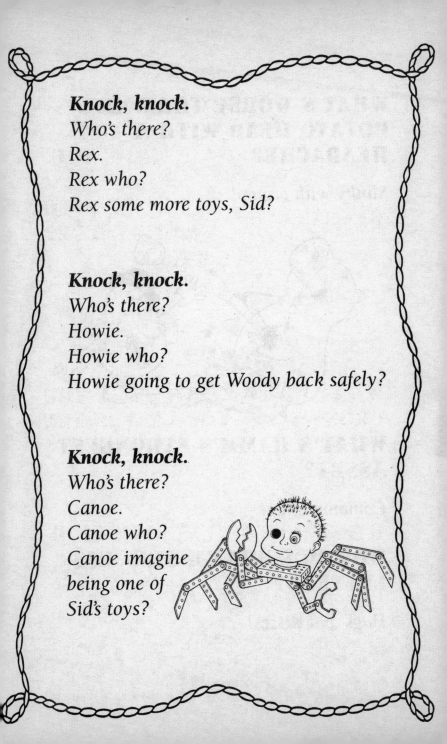

WHAT'S WORSE THAN MR POTATO HEAD WITH A HEADACHE?

Slinky with cramp!

WHAT'S HAMM'S STRONGEST ASSET?

Common cents!

HOW DOES HAMM SIGN HIS LETTERS?

Hogs and Kisses!

WHICH SIDE OF REX HAS THE MOST SCALES?

The outside!

WHY WAS SLINKY AFRAID OF BULLSEYE?

He thought he was a nightmare!

WHAT STARS DOES SHERIFF WOODY PUT IN JAIL?

Shooting stars!

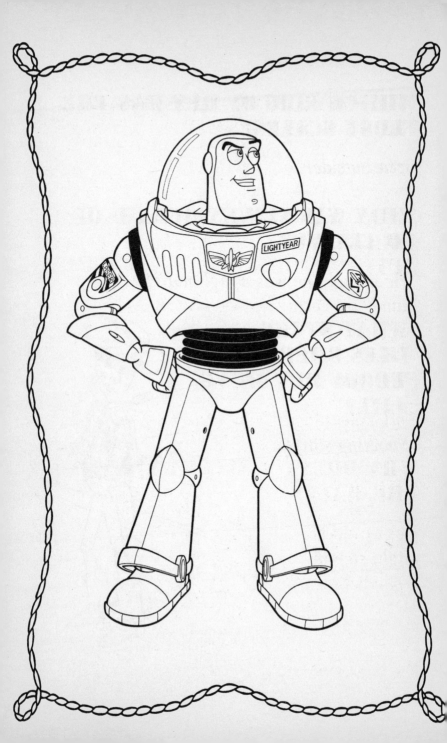

WHY DOES BUZZ LIGHTYEAR FLY IN A SPACESHIP?

Because trains are too slow!

WHAT KIND OF SANDWICHES DO THE BUZZ LIGHTYEAR ACTION FIGURES EAT?

Launching meat sandwiches!

WHAT DID BUZZ LIGHTYEAR SEE ON THE STOVE?

An Unidentified Frying Object!

WHY DOESN'T SLINKY LIKE THE RAIN?

He's afraid he might step in a poodle!

WHERE WOULD REX GO IF HE LOST HIS TAIL?

A re-tail shop!

WHAT WOULD REX NEED IF HE STUBBED HIS TOE?

A toe truck!

HOW CAN YOU TELL IF REX HAS BEEN IN YOUR REFRIGERATOR?

His footprints are in the butter!

WHAT MAKES REX AT THE BEACH SEEM LIKE CHRISTMAS?

His sandy claws!

WHY DID REX CROSS THE ROAD?

To prove he wasn't a chicken!

WHY IS WOODY SO COOL?

He has lots of fans!

Knock, knock.
Who's there?
Woody.
Woody who?
Woody really live
in a museum?

Knock, knock.
Who's there?
Bo.
Bo who?
Don't cry. Woody
will come back!

Knock, knock.
Who's there?
Al.
Al who?
Al have to ask Andy
if I can play with Woody.

WHAT DO YOU CALL HAMM STANDING BETWEEN WOODY AND BO?

A Hamm sandwich!

HOW DO YOU KEEP MR POTATO HEAD FROM SMELLING?

Take away his nose!

WHAT'S PINK AND FAT AND GOES UP AND DOWN?

Hamm in a lift!

WHAT SHOULD HAMM DO FOR A MUSCLE ACHE?

Rub on some oinkment!

WHY DID WOODY HAVE A LOT TO SAY?

Because Andy kept pulling his string!

WHAT IS ETCH'S CLAIM TO FAME?

He is the fastest draw in the West!

WHAT IS BUZZ LIGHTYEAR'S FAVOURITE RESTAURANT?

Pizza Planet!

WHAT'S THE MOST IMPORTANT MEETING IN ANDY'S ROOM?

The Plastic Corrosion Awareness Meeting!

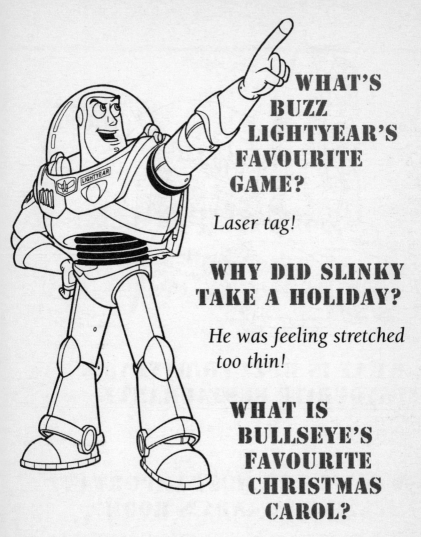

WHAT'S BUZZ LIGHTYEAR'S FAVOURITE GAME?

Laser tag!

WHY DID SLINKY TAKE A HOLIDAY?

He was feeling stretched too thin!

WHAT IS BULLSEYE'S FAVOURITE CHRISTMAS CAROL?

'Deck the Stalls with Boughs of Holly!'

WHAT IS SLINKY'S FAVOURITE CHRISTMAS CAROL?

'We Three Springs!'

WHAT GOES STEP, STEP, STEP, 'OUCH!'?

Prospector backing into a cactus!

WHAT GOES 'NEIGH', 'SPLASH', 'NEIGH', 'SPLASH'?

Bullseye crossing a stream!

HOW DO YOU HIDE REX ON A SNOOKER TABLE?

Make him wear a green hat!

DID YOU EVER SEE REX ON A SNOOKER TABLE?

NO?

See, it works!

Knock, knock.
Who's there?
Orange.
Orange who?
Orange you glad
Woody was saved?

Knock, knock.
Who's there?
Gladys.
Gladys who?
Gladys not me
who got kidnapped!

Knock, knock.
Who's there?
Dozen.
Dozen who?
Dozen anyone know how to find Al's
Toy Barn?

WHY DID SLINKY CROSS THE ROAD?

It was the chicken's day off!

HOW WOULD HAMM DRESS FOR A FORMAL RODEO?

Hog-tied!

WHY DID PROSPECTOR WEAR A THREE-PIECE SUIT?

He thought it was the wild, wild vest!

WHAT VEGETABLE DO YOU GET WHEN BULLSEYE GALLOPS THROUGH YOUR GARDEN?

Squash!

WHAT DOES MR POTATO HEAD WEAR TO BED?

His yammies!

WHAT IS BUZZ LIGHTYEAR'S FAVOURITE DESSERT?

Moon pies!

HOW DO YOU GET A BABY BUZZ LIGHTYEAR DOLL TO SLEEP?

You rocket!

HOW DO YOU MAKE BUZZ LIGHTYEAR STEW?

Keep him waiting for hours!

WHY DID REX BRING PLASTERS TO THE PICNIC?

He heard there were going to be cold cuts!

WHY DOES PROSPECTOR USE A PICKAXE TO LOOK FOR GOLD?

Because a fork would take too long!

WHAT IS SLINKY'S FAVOURITE SEASON?

Spring!

WHAT TIME IS IT WHEN WOODY, BUZZ, SLINKY, BO AND REX CHASE SCUD AND SID?

Five after two!

WHAT DO YOU GET WHEN YOU CROSS BO WITH THE RADIO-CONTROLLED CAR?

Someone who rounds up sheep really fast!

WHAT WOULD YOU CALL BO IF SHE GOT SICK?

A germy shepherd!

Knock, knock.
Who's there?
Hope.
Hope who?
Hope Woody and
the other toys got
back safely!

Knock, knock.
Who's there?
Noah.
Noah who?
Noah wild west
town where we
can find a
dinosaur?

Knock, knock.
Who's there?
Carl.
Carl who?
Carl a doctor! Woody's hurt his arm!

HOW DOES ANDY KNOW WHEN ALL HIS TOYS ARE UNDER HIS BED?

His nose touches the ceiling!

WHY DID JESSIE EAT A SANDWICH WHILE WALKING ON A FENCE?

She wanted a well-balanced diet!

WHY DO PEOPLE THINK THAT BULLSEYE IS DISAGREEABLE?

He's always saying 'nay'!

HOW DO YOU GET DOWN FROM REX?

You don't get down from dinosaurs, silly, you get down from ducks!

WHY DID HAMM LIKE THE RODEO?

Because he could go hog wild!

WHAT WOULD YOU CALL REX IF HE FELL IN THE MUD, THEN CROSSED A ROAD TWICE?

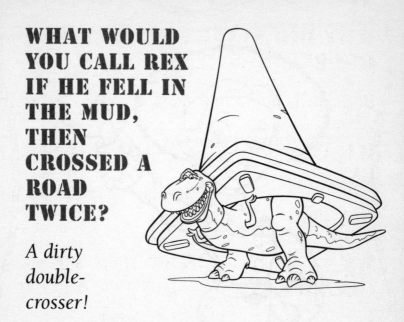

A dirty double-crosser!

HOW DO YOU KEEP HAMM FROM SMELLING?

GIVE HIM A BATH?

Nope, hold his nose!

WHY DID SLINKY FEEL LIKE A PUPPY?

Because he had a new leash on life!

WHAT IS SLINKY'S FAVOURITE CITY?

New Yorkie!

WHAT DOES SLINKY USE TO CLEAN UP?

Shampoodle!

WHY DID WOODY ASK MR POTATO HEAD TO BE A LOOKOUT?

Because he's all eyes!

WHY DID BUZZ TAKE A CAR DOOR INTO OUTER SPACE?

So he could roll down the window if he got too hot!

WHERE DOES REX BUY HIS CLOTHING?

At the dino-store!

PROSPECTOR:

'I keep seeing gold coins in front of my eyes.'

JESSIE:

'Have you seen the doctor?'

PROSPECTOR:

'No, just gold coins!'

WHAT'S COWBOY WOODY'S FAVOURITE KITCHEN APPLIANCE?

The range!

WHY DID HAMM EAT THE FLASHBULB?

He wanted a light snack!

WHAT IS BIG AND GREEN AND HAS FOUR WHEELS?

Rex on a skateboard!

WHAT MAKES SLINKY LIKE A TREE?

His bark!

WHY DO BO'S SHEEP WEAR BELLS ON THEIR NECKS?

Because their horns don't work!

WHY DOES HAMM STAY AWAY FROM TOADS?

He doesn't want to become a warthog!

WHAT ARE THE ONLY TWO THINGS THAT HAMM WON'T EAT FOR DINNER?

Breakfast and lunch!

WHY DID SLINKY CROSS THE ROAD?

To get to the barking lot!

Knock, knock.
Who's there?
Buzz Justin.
Buzz Justin who?
Buzz Justin time to rescue Woody!

Knock, knock.
Who's there?
Amos.
Amos who?
Amos to the stars, Buzz, it's time to
blast out of here!

Knock, knock.
Who's there?
Jessie.
Jessie who?
Jessie how far
Buzz flew?

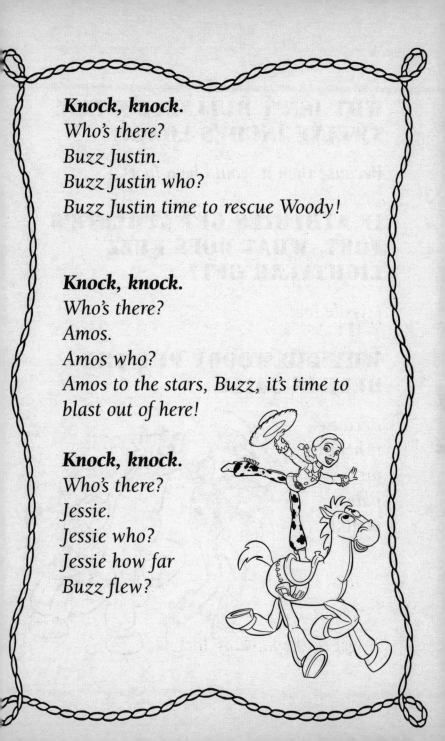

WHY ISN'T BULLSEYE'S TAIL TWELVE INCHES LONG?

Because then it would be a foot!

IF ATHLETES GET ATHLETE'S FOOT, WHAT DOES BUZZ LIGHTYEAR GET?

Missile toe!

WHY DID WOODY PUT THE BELT IN JAIL?

Because it held up a pair of pants!

WHY DID BUZZ ENJOY HIS ROCKET SHIP RIDE?

Because it was a real blast!

WHY DID BUZZ KEEP HIS SPACESHIP'S COMPUTER WARM?

He didn't want it to catch a virus!

WHAT DID BO SAY TO THE PHOTOGRAPHER?

'Some day my prints will come.'

WHAT WOULD YOU CALL EMPEROR ZURG WEARING EARMUFFS?

Anything you like. He can't hear you!

WHY IS HAMM SUCH A GOOD FRIEND TO HAVE IN AN EMERGENCY?

Because you can really count on his good cents.

WHY DOES BUZZ NEED TO HIRE MORE HELP?

Because he fired his rocket!

WHAT DO YOU CALL MR AND MRS POTATO HEAD'S KIDS?

Chips off the old block!

WHAT IS BUZZ'S FAVOURITE KEY ON A COMPUTER KEYBOARD?

The space bar!

WHAT TIME IS IT WHEN TEN COWBOYS CHASE THREE BANDITS?

Ten after three!

WHAT TIME IS IT WHEN TEN BANDITS CHASE WOODY?

Time to get help!

WHAT DID THE LITTLE GREEN ALIENS SAY TO THE NEWSPAPER?

'Take me to your reader!'

WHAT DO YOU CALL SLINKY WHEN HE'S CROSS?

A hot dog!

WHAT DO YOU CALL HAMM'S LAUNDRY?

Hogwash!

WHAT DID EMPEROR ZURG SAY TO THE PARKED CAR?

'Take me to your meter!'

WHY DID THE PROSPECTOR BRING A MATHS BOOK TO WOODY'S RODEO?

He heard there'd be some rounding up!

WHAT SHOULD YOU SAY TO PROSPECTOR WHEN HE'S ON THE ROOF OF A BARN?

'Get down!'

WHERE DOES BULLSEYE STAY IN A HOTEL?

The bridle suite!

WHY DID JESSIE PUT SLINKY NEAR THE CAMPFIRE?

Because Woody said he wanted a hot dog!

WHAT DID THE LITTLE GREEN ALIENS SAY TO THE FLOWER GARDEN?

'Take me to your weeder!'

WHY DOESN'T SLINKY SPEAK TO HIS FOOT?

Because it's not polite to talk back to your paw!

WHY DID REX STARE AT THE ORANGE JUICE CONTAINER FOR FIFTEEN MINUTES?

Because it said 'concentrate'!

Knock, knock.
Who's there?
Lettuce.
Lettuce who?
Lettuce in! Emperor Zurg is after us!

Knock, knock.
Who's there?
Ivana.
Ivana who?
Ivana see Toy Story 2 again!

Knock, knock.
Who's there?
Dismay.
Dismay who?
Dismay be the last joke about
Toy Story 2!

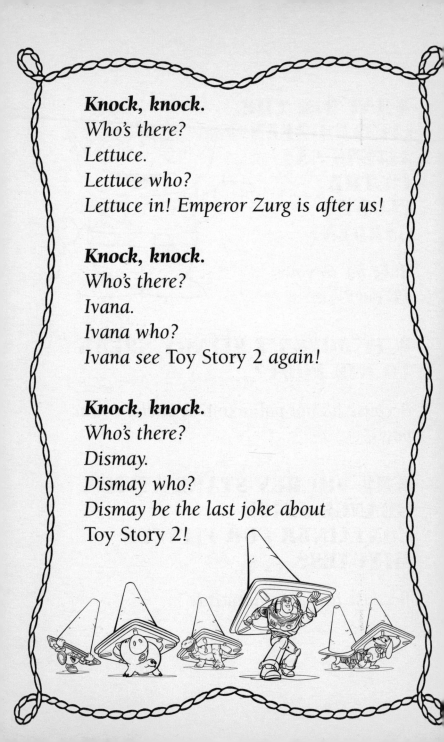